OBSERVATIONS

Upon a late

LIBEL

1681

OBSERVATIONS

Upon a late LIBEL, called

A Letter from a Person of Quality
to his Friend, concerning the

King's Declaration, *&c*

Edited, with an Introduction
and Bibliography
by
HUGH MACDONALD

CAMBRIDGE
At the Univerſity Preſs
MCMXL

CAMBRIDGE
UNIVERSITY PRESS

University Printing House, Cambridge CB2 8BS, United Kingdom

Cambridge University Press is part of the University of Cambridge.

It furthers the University's mission by disseminating knowledge in the pursuit of education, learning and research at the highest international levels of excellence.

www.cambridge.org
Information on this title: www.cambridge.org/9781107585768

© Cambridge University Press 1940

First published 1940
First paperback edition 2015

A catalogue record for this publication is available from the British Library

ISBN 978-1-107-58576-8 Paperback

INTRODUCTION

No statesman who has taken a prominent part
in guiding this country during periods of extreme
difficulty has written with so much wisdom and
eloquence as the Marquis of Halifax. Little
record of his speeches remains, but his writings
have as much significance for our time as for his
own and his style has an ease and informality
which is rare in the political literature left us by
men who have been famous for their oratory.
A well-known passage, which it is difficult to
resist quoting at the present time, will serve as
an example. 'I will make no other Introduction
to the following Discourse, than that as the
Importance of our being strong at Sea was ever
very great, so in our present Circumstances, it is
grown to be much greater; because as formerly
our Force of Shipping contributed greatly to our
Trade and Safety, so now it is become indis-
pensably necessary to our very Being. It may be
said now to England, *Martha, Martha*, thou
art busy about many things, but one thing is
necessary to the Question, What shall we do
to be saved in this World? There is no other
Answer but this, Look to your Moate. The first
Article of an *English-mans* Political Creed must

be, That he believeth in the Sea, without that there needeth no General Council, to pronounce him incapable of Salvation here.'

I believe *Observations upon a late Libel* to have been written by Halifax, but hastily and for an immediate purpose. It is not on the continuously high level of *A Rough Draught of a New Model at Sea*, or *The Character of a Trimmer* : it has more in common with *Some Cautions for Choice of Members in Parliament* and *Political Thoughts and Reflections*. It is witty and effective and, if I am right in ascribing it to him, it is worth rescuing and adding to the small body of his work.

The Cavalier Parliament, which had been elected in 1661, was dissolved in January 1679 and was succeeded by the first Whig Parliament, as it is called, which sat from March till May and was dissolved in July 1679. The refusal or omission of this body to re-enact the Press Act made it easier for a time than it had been to publish news-sheets and pamphlets hostile to the Government. The second Whig Parliament, though returned in the Autumn of 1679, sat only from October 1680 till January 1681. In this parliament a bill to exclude the Duke of York from the Throne was rejected in the Lords, where it was eloquently opposed by the Earl of Halifax, as he then was, and the Commons subsequently voted an address to the King for the Earl's removal from His Majesty's presence and councils. The last parliament of Charles II's reign sat at Oxford from 21 to 28 March 1681. The Whigs, who were outwitted by the sudden dissolution, though now powerless, were very angry, and it was thought expedient to publish *His Majesties Declaration To all His Loving Subjects Touching the Causes That moved him to Dissolve the Two last Parliaments.* This is dated 8 April, although, in one of the replies to it, *A Just and Modest Vindication of the proceedings of the Two last Parliaments,* probably by Robert Ferguson (see *Robert Ferguson the Plotter,* 1887), it is said that Barillon, the French Ambassador, had seen it two days earlier. Another reply to the King was *A Letter from a Person of Quality to his Friend concerning His Majesties late Declaration,* which probably came out at the end of April (*Cal. State Papers Dom.* 1680–1, 260). This was answered by Dryden in *His Majesties Declaration Defended* (no. 129 of my Dryden Bibliography). It was also answered by *Observations upon a late Libel.*

Directly after the Oxford Parliament had ended Halifax went on a visit to his uncle, Sir William Coventry, at Bibury, and on 4 April he left there for his own seat at Rufford, where he remained, possibly with a view to retiring from public life altogether, till he was recalled to the King by an urgent letter from Sir Leoline Jenkins written on 19 May (*Cal. State Papers Dom.* 1680–1, 287). The author of *Observations* says that *A Letter from a Person of Quality* reached him

'with other Pamphlets...in the country' and he
implies that the answer is being written in the
country. A difficulty may arise here for I have
not found a reference to *Observations* before
30 July, when it was advertised in *The Observator*,
but it may have been written and even printed
some time before this, as Dryden's pamphlet is
also advertised in the same number, although it
had been discussed in that paper on 22 June.
My attention was first called to the possibility
of Halifax being the author of *Observations* by
the existence of a copy in the library of Trinity
College, Cambridge, which has 'By ye E. of
Hallifax' added in manuscript under the title.
Manuscript notes of this kind on seventeenth-
century tracts must be accepted with caution, but
in this instance I attach considerable importance
to it. I judge the handwriting to be of about
1680 and, moreover, Savile was Earl of Halifax
only from July 1679 till August 1682. None
of the pamphlets now known to be his had been
published at this time, so it is probable that
whoever inserted his name had something other
than the style of the piece to go on. Charles
Montague cannot have been intended as he was
not created Earl of Halifax till 1715.

The internal evidence for Halifax seems to me
to be very strong: indeed, if he did not write
it, he must have had a literary double. It is
difficult to think of anyone else of the time to
whom it can be attributed. Sir William Coventry

was a country gentleman, who approved of the King's *Declaration* (Foxcroft, 1, 296). He had considerable influence over his nephew and he was for some years thought to have been the author of *The Character of a Trimmer*, but it would be the merest guesswork to suggest that he wrote *Observations*. The tract is evidently the work of someone who writes with authority and is also evidently not by a professional pamphleteer. A disproportionate amount of space is given to the vote of the Commons, and Sir Henry Capel, who had spoken violently against Halifax, is mentioned with sarcasm. It *may* be of significance that in referring to the votes, the writer slips into the first person singular 'lieth in him to kill me'. But it is not so much from indications of this sort that I attribute the piece to Halifax as from the similarity of its style to his accepted writings. *Observations* seems to have the characteristic turn of his sentences, his marked rhythm and several of his idiosyncrasies.

One of these is his constant use of the termination *-th* for the third person singular, and although one occasionally finds this archaism elsewhere at the end of the seventeenth century, particularly in letters, it would be difficult to find a parallel to the sentence in the second paragraph 'If the Court maketh' as late as 1680. A striking example of his vocabulary is the use of the word 'right' for 'justice', a habit of Halifax to which Miss Foxcroft called attention.

We have 'to do these men right' and 'do the King right to the People', cf. 'To do Right to these fine-spun Gentlemen' (Raleigh 153). Political catch-phrases which occur in *Observations* can be found if one turns the pages of Raleigh's edition, e.g. 'angry men', 'Peace and Union' and 'Men of Law'. The remark 'That no man who is a known Ass in his own business, may be thought fit to meddle with the Kings' is very like Halifax's 29th *Maxim of State* 'That a Man who cannot mind his own Business, is not to be trusted with the Kings'. The passage on p. 20 referring to the Popish Plot 'Ungrateful men then, that speak ill of the only thing in this world that supporteth them' may be compared with 'others that must have Plots...and have an interest to keep them alive, since they are to live upon them' (Raleigh 100). In the last paragraph the words 'to see *England* look like itself again' strike a note familiar to those who know *The Character of a Trimmer*. Besides verbal parallels and similarities of thought, which separately go for little, but together form valuable evidence, the arguments seem to me to be presented in a manner that is typical of Halifax. Instead of vituperation and direct attack there is sharpness of wit, subtlety and irony, and if there is not the freedom from personalities that one associates with him it must be remembered that he was smarting under what he considered an unjustifiable attack.

It has been suggested to me that the arguments are in too conventional a Tory vein for Halifax. But the pamphlet begins with what is, in fact, a complaint of the extravagance of parties, one of his favourite themes; it is an answer to the Whig case; he was capable of changing his opinions on the practical conduct of affairs with considerable rapidity and he was at this time supporting the Court. Miss Foxcroft and later historians have been inclined to believe that he had a hand in the King's speech at the opening of the Oxford Parliament. *The Character of a Trimmer*, in which he expounds his considered political principles, was, after all, written more than three years later. That *Observations* was not included in *Miscellanies*, 1700, or mentioned in the manuscript *Saviliana*, reprinted in various parts of Miss Foxcroft's volumes, is, I think, of little importance. The writer of such a piece could easily print it without anyone discovering who he was. Even Dryden's pamphlet has only recently been generally recognised as his.

Everyone interested in Halifax is under an obligation to Miss H. C. Foxcroft, whose *Life and Letters of Halifax* is and will remain our chief source of information about him. Her edition gives us a better text than Raleigh's; but her volumes are not always to be obtained and a new edition of his writings may some day be wanted. I have therefore added a bibliography of those editions which an editor would be likely to need, three of which Miss Foxcroft had not seen.

I have used the symbol π for the title-leaves in the collations of $3e$ and g, though possibly the frontispiece and title-leaf form sig. [A]^2.

I should like to thank Mr Basil Willey, Mr E. S. de Beer, Miss G. Lloyd Thomas and Miss M. C. Bradbrook for help they have given me.

H. M.

OBSERVATIONS

Upon a late LIBEL, called

A Letter from a Person of Quality to his Friend, concerning the

Kings Declaration, &c

WE live in an Age where ill humor and Malice to the Government do fo prevail, that men rail without any manner of diftinction, and without examining what things are good or bad in themfelves ; there feemeth to be no other Rule allowed by one fort of Men, than that they cannot Err, and the King cannot be in the Right : This general Maxim is fo eafie, by taking the trouble of any further enquiry, that no wonder if it is cherifhed and entertained ; and thofe who are fo prepoffeffed, are ready to turn the beft things to a wrong fenfe, and to receive fuch an interpretation of every thing that comes from the Court, as their Mifleaders are pleafed to impofe upon them.

The Wifer fort of them knowing nothing is fo deftructive to their ends, as that the Government fhould take fuch meafures as might filence their Objections, have an intereft to blaft every thing that is done on that fide, and to disfigure with the colours they put upon them, all fuch things as might undeceive the People, and reconcile them to the Crown; for at the fame time they appear fo eager to have Grievances redreffed, their more fecret Prayers are that they may be increafed: If the Court maketh any falfe fteps, or giveth any provocation, it raifeth Noife and Clamour, the voice againft it is loud; but the killing grief that afflicteth them inwardly, and galleth them to the foul, is, when the King doth a gracious or a plaufible Act to the Publick.

Of this there cannot be a greater inftance than their being fo afflicted at the Kings late Declaration: It was an evidence of their grief, that it was fo long before they anfwered it: It was received with a filent indignation that the Court fhould prefume to out-argue them; and though they had rage enough to rail, yet they were for fome time reftrained from their ufual Dialect by the reverence that is due to Reafon, even when it is contrary to our Paffions or Interefts.

At laft when they faw the effect it had in the Nation, and being not without reafon apprehenfive, that mens eyes might be fo opened as to fee them through their popular Difguife, they thought of two ills, it was advifable to chufe the leaft; and rather than lie under the general reproach of having nothing to fay, they chofe to venture a Reply, though they could not make a good one, prefuming upon the fuccefs they had met with in their impofing upon the world, and believing it would be fo favourably difpofed on

their fide, that where their falfe Arguments could
not pafs, they would at leaft be connived at.

This being after more than one Meeting refolved at a Confult, out cometh a Letter to a
Friend, which of late fignifieth little lefs than a
Proclamation fet out by the Authority of the
high and mighty Confervators of *England*, there is
only this difference which is for their advantage,
that if thefe Letters take in the world, they are
imputed to the wifdom of thefe great Governors;
if not, they are eafily laid upon fome foolifh
fellow that would be fcribling; by which means
the veneration due to thefe Princes of the People
remains unblemifhed and entire.

This coming with other Pamphlets to me in
the Country, I was tempted to make fome fhort
Obfervations which are fubmitted to the cenfure
of the unbyaffed Reader. Firft they are troubled,
that though Parliaments are frequent, they are
fhort and ufelefs.

The King hath done his part in calling Parliaments often, for which he is to be thanked;
except it can be made evident it was his fault
that they were of no longer continuance: fo far
from that, it is plain thefe men who complain have
been fo much the caufe of the late Diffolutions,
that one would fwear they defigned to provoke
the King to them, and that he hath had in thefe
cafes fo much patience, he can hardly anfwer it
to the Nation, whofe peace he is entrufted with
and bound to preferve.

The Exceſſes of the Commons were beyond the cure of lower Remedies, and there was no other choice left, than either to part with the Parliament, or let the two Houſes continue ſitting in a ſtate of Hoſtility hardly poſſible to be reconciled ; of which the conſequences are ſo obvious, and might have been ſo fatal, that we are to thank God the Conſtitution of the Government hath lodged this neceſſary Power in the Crown to preſerve us from Ruine upon ſuch occaſions.

But fain they would have Parliaments ſit as long as they pleaſe, and I cannot blame them, Authority is ſweet ; and a Member of Parliament that would have us believe he bringeth all the ſenſe of his Country or Corporation along with him, cometh to teach the King better manners, and to adviſe him to keep better company. I ſay for ſuch a dignified Creature as this is, by one word of the Kings mouth to be reduced into his own ſingle ſelf again, is ſo cruel a change, that no wonder if men ſo degraded are angry at it, and would be glad, inſtead of being as little men as their Neighbors, to gain that ſuperiority which Nature denied them, by virtue of an Authority to continue for their lives.

It ſeemeth then by this, that a long Parliament is not in it ſelf a Grievance, for now they would have one that they think their Party ſhall prevail in it.

And it is obſervable that thoſe who were for the firſt Long Parliament, and againſt the ſecond,

are now the chief men that would have a third:
How far this fhould recommend the opinion
either to the King or the Nation, I leave every
man to judge; but to do thefe men right, they
are for the prefent fo modeft they will not fpeak
out, fo I will do it for them.

The little thing they would have is a Houfe
of Commons that may do what they will, how
they will, and as long as they will, that is for
ever, whether the King liveth or dieth, they muft
not be difcompofed, nor their Authority inter-
rupted, for I would fain know where lieth the
real difference between having a Parliament fit
for ever, or till all Grievances are redreffed: the
diftinction will be very nice in an Age where it
is Treafon againft the People not to grumble
againft the Government. Thefe rich Mines of
Fears and Jealoufies can never be exhaufted in
our time, fo that the Workmen are fure not only
to be employed for their lives, but to fecure their
Pofterities being fo after them.

The Monarchy in the mean time would be in
a good cafe to be under the continual Wardfhip of
fuch fevere Guardians; and thefe very Gentlemen who have upon another occafion affirmed
that the very name of King muft of neceffity carry
the authority along with it, would not fail to give
a full inftance to the contrary, if they could ever
catch our Mafter in the Net of a Perpetual
Parliament.

They are troubled that the Declaration fhould

be read in Churches, from which this Obfervation naturally arifeth, that they apprehend the making it fo publick, may both expofe them, and do the King right to the People; elfe fure they would not of a fuddain be fo well natured, as to difcourage the reading it, if they had thought the weaknefs of the Argument might have brought any difadvantage upon the King.

This Paper hath laid down Maxims that are very new in our Conftitution, *The King can make no ill Orders becaufe they muft be by advice of his Council.* This is a new Government, and the Monarchy put fo much into the *Venetian* fhape, that a man would have much ado to diftinguifh them.

It will be granted that the King is to hear the Advice of his Council, but for him to be bound by it, would make that greater than the Parliament; where if the King hath right to refufe any Bill that is offered, fure he may in Council rejeÉ any Opinion. I am confident it is not their meaning to attribute fuch an Authority to the prefent Council; I am perfuaded it is far from their thoughts to wifh the King fhould be fwayed by a number of men who are fo little in their favour, and efpecially fince it wanteth the help of thofe whofe abilities and other Vertues in their opinion did formerly fupport it. This Complement muft therefore be intended for another Council, a confiding Council that is to be made up with the reft of the New Model, we may fuppofe is prepared againſt the *Bill of Excluſion* is paſs'd, and then they do not care how much power they give to themſelves, or take away from the King.

To excuſe the not giving Money for *Tangier*, they pretend they could not be ſecure of its being diſpoſed to that uſe. It is hard they ſhould expect the world ſhould believe them in this, when it is certain they do not believe themſelves. The experience we have had in our own time may ſufficiently convince them of the injuſtice of that Objection; and to ſay Paper Laws are nothing, is to ſay our Liberties and Properties are nothing, ſince we hold them chiefly by that tenure: But the truth is, theſe men would impoſe upon us, that an Act of Parliament will ſecure nothing they do not like, and do every thing they have a mind to: For inſtance, *An Act for excluding the Duke is all-ſufficient. An Act for limiting him Impoſſible. An Act of Excluſion will ſecure all. All other Laws are but Cobwebs not to be relied upon.* Theſe Riddles are delivered to us with ſuch authority, that we are to receive them as Oracles, and it is become a mortal ſin for any man to queſtion the ſenſe of them.

This ſlender way of reaſoning being ſo openly liable to confutation, and the diſguiſe ſo thin that every body muſt ſee through it, they have recourſe to that common place, the *PLOT*, for a Butterefs and a ſupport to Arguments that are too weak to bear up themſelves.

It is a retreat when they are beaten in Diſpute,

an anfwer to any queftion at a pinch; it is but
faying there is a horrid Plot againft our Religion,
the Kings Life is in danger, the Pilgrims are
coming from St. *Jago*, and the Earl of *Shaftsbury*
is to be murthered, and the Popular Champion
triumpheth without the help of Senfe, againft
his Adverfary. That there hath been a Plot, is
as certain, as that the men who moft exclaim
againft it are of all men living the moft unwilling
to part with it: they cherifh and nurfe it up with
more care than the Jefuites themfelves; they
hug it fo faft, that it fheweth how much they
value it, as the dear inftrument they make ufe
of to deftroy the Government. The Day of
Judgment would not be much more terrible to
fome men, how little foever they are prepared
for it, than that day which fhould wind up the
bottom of this beloved Plot, that men might
come into their wits again. Ungrateful men then,
that fpeak ill of the only thing in this world that
fupporteth them: But the good men in their
hearts are far from meaning it any harm. Were
the Plot once over, the Earl of *Shaftsbury* would
be quite degraded, lofe his refpect at *Wapping*,
and his authority in the Coffee-Houfes. His
Lordfhip would put off his diffembling-fhape,
and in this be a true mourner: for never man
could have a greater lofs, and no doubt it would
out of grief make him retire into fome hidden
corner, rather than fee himfelf reduced to the
miferable neceffity of being quiet for want of

fufficient matter to trouble himfelf and the world with; fo that when thefe men pretend to defire an end of the Plot, it is a Jeft fitter for a Smile than an Anfwer.

It is faid *Dangerfield* was a Rogue, granted, and yet as I hear, this Rogue was brought into both Houfes juft before the Debate, to whip them up into the *Bill of Exclufion*, but now they tell a very ftrange thing, which is, that *Dangerfield* is become truly honeft. It is much, and in my opinion, it is a lower kind of Tranfubftantiation to believe *Dangerfield* is honeft, when nothing is vifible but the Knave. That this man fhould be made honeft would be a mighty Cure, and fuch a one as fome of his Doctors would be loth to work upon themfelves. In the mean time I cannot but put them in mind that it looketh a little Popifh, not only to give a general Indulgence to fuch a known finner, but immediately to make a Saint of him. If the Gathered Churches can do fuch Miracles, it is well, but if they fhould endeavour to put falfe ones upon the world, it might difparage their prudence, and leffen their reputation; of which I am fo tender, that in kindnefs to them I give them this warning of it.

It is true that in fome refpects the Maxim is not inconvenient for thefe good men, *That there can be neither Fools nor Rafcals on their fide, and that the being of their opinion, like the Crown, taketh away all Defects:* By virtue of this charm Dr. *Oats* is a Divine, Mr. *Mountague* a Proteftant, Lord

Lovelace a Saint, Sir *Thomas Armstrong* a Patriot, and Sir *Harry Capel* a Statesman.

I cannot but take notice of the fears the Earl of *Shaftsbury* hath for himself, and in good nature would be glad to ease him of them; in order to it, I beg of him to believe the Papists are as tender of his life, as his Lordship is of the Plot: and for the same reason, because he is of use to them, he hath absolutely saved them by spoiling a good Plot, and dressing it so scurvily by the help of his under-Cook, that now it maketh even the best mens stomachs rise at it. He serveth up things so much above the strongest digestion, that few men can be persuaded to swallow them. So that a man may affirm, that if it was a folly in the Papists to kill Sir *Edmond Godfrey*, it would be a madness in them to hurt the Earl of *Shaftsbury*.

These Gentlemen are angry with the Guards which are so illegally kept up. Pray since when are they judged so? is it only since the Duke of *Monmouth* was put away from them? strange! that since that time there must be such a change, that he must be made lawful, and they illegal. It must be confessed, that next to the Laws, the Guards are the things of the world these men most hate: Fie upon them naughty fellows, they stand between them and home. The good men would fain have a safe victory, and do their business without venturing their skulls. For would it not be a cruel thing for an honest well-meaning Mutineer for his Zeal to destroy the Government, whilſt he is about it, to have his brains knockt out, and ſo loſe the benefit of ſpoiling the Ægyptians. Verily it is much better to have the Guards down, that he may walk into *Whitehal* with leſs peril of his perſon, and help to remove the Dukes Creatures out of all places Military and Civil.

For be it known to all men by theſe preſents, that the Duke is more dangerous to us as he is the Great Miniſter of State, than as he is the next Succeſſor. Say you ſo, Gentlemen, men gueſſed before this was your meaning; but I am ſorry for your ſakes you are ſo unwary as to diſcover it: Why ſuch earneſtneſs to remove the Succeſſor, when the danger is confeſſed to be greater from the Miniſter? Come, ſpeak out, the Poſition is, The Duke governeth all; conſequently every man in employment is his Creature, for that they are to be turned out, and theſe Gentlemen taken in: the deſign is well enough laid, and would do them more good than the *Bill of Excluſion*, which is but a pretence, and a thing fitted for other ends: But they did not do well to blab this out before it was time, it is a thouſand pities the Scheme ſhould not take, but I very much doubt it as things now ſtand, which is to be lamented, that the good men ſhould have taken ſo much pains, and all likely to be to ſo little purpoſe.

After having arraigned the Declaration, they come to juſtifie the proceedings of the Commons in the two laſt Meetings, and ſpeaking of ſome of their Addreſſes, ſay, *The nature, and true ſtate of Affairs would not bear a milder way of repreſenting things to his Majeſty.* Let them ſpeak truth, was it not rather the nature of thoſe men, whoſe pride and anger made them delight in handling the King roughly, and perſuade the Houſe, when they were asked what ſhould be done with *Tangier*, to anſwer with Popery and a Remonſtrance.

In the mean time I admire the caution of thoſe *Wiſe* and *Good Men*, who as the Paper ſaith, *thought the Commons had gone too far, inſomuch as mentioning Money till our ſafety was fully provided for.* They muſt be very jealous that could ſuſpect any ſuch danger; for beſides that we are very ſafe in the management of thoſe that led the Houſe, who no doubt will ever have a moſt particular care of us in theſe caſes; one may aſſure the *Wiſe and Good Men* of a further and better ſecurity, which is, that the Government is not yet ſo low as to ſell it ſelf ſo cheap. As for what the Commons propoſed, when-ever they have a mind to deal, it is to be hoped they will offer ſome more equal Bargain, than to demand from the King the whole power of the Crown both Civil and Military, and to propoſe from themſelves things ſo general, and ſo low, that the Supreme Wiſdom of the Nation could hardly be thought in earneſt when they offered them.

It is added for a further excuſe that jealouſies eaſily ariſe amongſt Numbers, which is enough to hinder any intended Agreement. The anſwer to this is, that it is true, there did arife fome jealoufies, that the Promoters of an Agreement with the King did not forget themfelves in it; but the Gentlemen who were concerned being fenfible of it, did for their Vindication procure a folemn Vote, That no Member of the Houfe fhould receive any place from the King *without the leave of the Houfe*, which was fo perfect a cure for jealoufie, that they are unjuft to be againft all expedients, after this had been fo profperous. I am half in a rapture, when I think of this glorious Vote, worthy to be written in Letters of Gold, and impoffible ever to be enough commended: By the firft part of it they fhewed their felf-denial, and by their fecond their deference to a Houfe they thought at leaft they governed. Great men fure they muft be, and bleffed with fo happy genius, that could fo mingle their Difcretion with their Generofity, as at once to gain honor, and provide for their intereft. The anfwer to the Kings Charge upon them for their Arbitrary Orders, is fo weak and faint, that it cometh very near a confeffion of their guilt in it, and it would be unkind to prefs them too hard in that which they themfelves feem to be afhamed of. I will only take notice of one expreffion, which is, *That they have erred with their Fathers*. If this is not true, it is no good Argument: and if it is true, they muft allow it to be as good a one for the Papifts, as it is for the Commons.

They come next to fupport their Votes againft

M O   4

particular perfons, and do very boldly affert it may
be made good by Law, *The King ought to have no
perfon near him who hath the misfortune of fuch a
Vote upon him.* Great Lawyers no doubt have their
part in this affertion : but they who in fo many
cafes difpute the Authority of the Crown, muft
allow men in this to demur to theirs ; and I am
troubled that a Vote of the Commons muft be
called a Misfortune ; becaufe it looketh as if chance
or fudden heat, rather than the deliberate Debates
and Juftice of the Houfe had produced it. Where
there is a fetled Rule, and that Right only pre-
vaileth, as mens guilt maketh them fall, fo their
innocence abfolveth them. But if men muft de-
pend upon their good or ill Stars, or upon the
wafpifh humor of an Affembly when an angry
Planet reigneth, the confequence is, that a man
though never fo faultlefs may by misfortune without guilt be transformed by a Vote, into an enemy
of King and Kingdom ; that is to fay, into a man
fit to be knocked on the head, and the Murtherer
to be rewarded as the Law formerly directed for
killing a Wolf ; and yet God forbid one fhould
think the Commons intended him any harm.

Well, but if the Houfe declareth they have
juft reafon to fear fuch or fuch a perfon dangerous,
muft there be Order and Procefs of Law before
he can be removed ?

When the Commons have juft reafon to fear
fuch a thing, it is to be hoped the whole Houfe
knoweth that juft reafon, or elfe they would not

Vote it: when-ever therefore they will tell that
juſt reaſon to the King, he is to blame in caſe he
findeth it ſo, if he doth not comply with them;
but if he judge otherwiſe, he hath as much right
to refuſe, as they can pretend to have to ask. But
if it muſt be ſo, that not only the real, but the
pretended fears of ſome angry men, who may have
influence enough to miſlead an Aſſembly not ſufficiently informed, are to have ſuch an Authority,
that the Kings Negative to them is diſallowed, it
is ſuch a change of the Conſtitution, that the
Legiſlative Power is wholly melted down into one
of the parts that hath yet no power to do any Act
that is binding without the concurrence of the
Lords, and the Kings Royal Aſſent.

This doth ſo much out-go even our modern
Plato, that it will be a harder matter than perhaps
theſe Gentlemen think, to get either the King or
the Nation to conſent to it. Men are not ſo well
edified with the practice of the Commons in this
laſt Age, or the juſtice that hath been uſually diſtri-
buted by their Sovereign Committees, as to de-
volve the whole power into their hands, thinking
it much better lodged where it is by the preſent
Conſtitution. But it is ſaid the Commons by their
late Methods do not fine men, nor deprive them
of Life, Liberty, Lands or Offices beneficial. I
would firſt ask, is it not a Fine, and to many men
the worſt kind of Fine, to be excluded from the
lawful advantages every Subject is born to. Would
not a Merchant think it a Fine, if he were ſen-

tenced never to go to Sea again? Or to come nearer, Would not thefe very men of Law who will have this pafs upon us, take it unkindly, and think it a Fine, if they were excluded from all Practice? 'Tis true, if they would always argue for their Clients, as they do now for the Commons, their lofs perhaps might not be very great; but prefuming better things of them, I conclude the fentence would be very heavy, and that they would think it fo.

Concerning Life, if the definition of an enemy to King and Kingdom is a certain creature that is not fit to live, then the Commons have done all they can to take away the lives of thofe they have fo fentenced, except they had fent a felect Committe[e] to ftrangle them, which had not been fo convenient till the Laws are removed, which would have made it Murther; fo that they muft either fay that a man who doth what lieth in him to kill me, meaneth no hurt to my life, which is but indifferent fenfe; or they muft confefs there was plain Murther in the intention of thofe Votes.

For to borrow their own ftile, it may be refolved by the authority of impartial reafon, that whofo-ever Voted any of thofe perfons enemies to King and Kingdom with any other intent than that the faid Perfons fhould be abfolutely deftroyed, is a Mad-man, an Ideot, a Promoter of Lunacy, and an enemy to Common Senfe.

Then for Liberty, fee whether that is touched

or no. If Liberty fignifieth a power of doing every
lawful act, and that it is a lawful act for every
Subject to have accefs to his Prince, then without
fome act committed to forfeit that common right,
it is a wrong in any one man, or any number of
men to Addrefs to the King for the incapacitating
any one man in this cafe. Sure men will not fay
our Liberty is not invaded except we are thrown
neck and heels into a Dungeon. It is a tenderer
thing than that cometh to, and it hath been formerly
judged even by a Houfe of Commons, that mens
being fent away againft their wills upon Forein
Employment, was a Confinement. By this it may
appear that it is poffible to make an unjuft Demand
as well as to give an unjuft Sentence : And though
the King hath power to refufe any thing that is
asked of him, whatever fome men would perfuade
us to the contrary, yet that doth neither abfolve
the Commons, nor any other man from the guilt
of making a requeft that is not juft, nor from the
folly of making one that is not pertinent.

Let us fee now whether even mens Lands would
not have been reached by thefe Votes, if thefe
good Gentlemen might have had their will; for
by the fame rule that a true Proteftant Jury muft
have been directed by them not to find it Murther
in any man to kill an enemy to King and Kingdom,
they muft upon any difpute of title of Land, give
it without going from the Bar againft any man fo
branded and proclaimed. Sure a *French* or *Dutch-
man*, at a time when they are in open War with

us, would hardly hope to carry a caufe againſt an *Engliſh-man* in *Weſtminſter-Hall* ; no more is a man to pretend, whilſt under a Character that putteth him into a ſtate of Hoſtility with *England*, to keep up a ſuit againſt a Neighbor, or expect the benefit of the Law, which is to give no protection to publick Enemies.

As to Offices beneficial, it muſt be confeſſed they ſhew ſome gentleneſs at laſt, and give ſo much indulgence to thoſe they have diſplaced by their Votes, that I do not ſee but any of them may upon due application, and expreſſive and fit remorſe for the inſolence of reſiſting their high and mighty pleaſure, be admitted to be a Conſtable or Head-borough in *Wales* or *Cumberland*, or ſome ſuch unexpected Office in which *the Publick State Affairs are not immediately concerned*, where they may exerciſe their Magiſtracy, and enjoy their dignity without prejudice to the Nation.

This Grace ſeemeth the fitter to be acknow-ledged, not only becauſe it is perhaps the firſt evidence that party hath given of their good nature, but becauſe they do in this deal more gently with thoſe againſt whom they have Voted, than they do with his Majeſty himſelf as well as they love him ; for by what I can perceive, the King is only to eat and drink, and perform ſome offices of nature. They are kind men ; but it was not artificially done to leave it out, that *A King is to have ſome Pocket-money for playthings*, ſince it is but reaſon-able for them to uſe a thing kindly, which if they

can have in their power, they intend to make so
good use of.

That wise and great Princes have sometimes
hearkened to Addresses of this kind, is not truer,
than that they have oftner denied them : for the
King to do in all cases like a wise and a great
Prince, as it is a general proposition, all who do
not know him have reason to wish it, and all who
do have very good grounds to hope it. But as
far as one sort of men may be concerned in their
own particulars, I guess wrong, if it would not
be too fatal a thing to them ever to joyn in Prayer
for it.

The Votes to forbid men to lend the King
money, are to these mens thinking not only
justifiable, but very wise ones too. These are
Epithetes which it seemeth belong to every thing
they do, or else I would ask where is the Justice
of doing that for which they have no authority,
or the Wisdom of doing that which hath no effect ;
only it sheweth their good will, by throwing the
greatest indignity they could upon the Government. Men will lend still notwithstanding this
mighty Vote, and perhaps upon easier terms than
these Gentlemen would require for any money
they part with in Parliament. In the mean time
would these equitable men take it well, if by their
example the King should send to all the Burroughs
and Counties in *England* not to chuse such and
such men, nor to trust those with a share in making
Laws, who have in the late Parliaments assumed

to themfelves the priviledge of breaking them? The argument is at leaft as ftrong on the Kings fide, without any Complement to Majefty, as they can pretend to make theirs, upon the pretence of diftruft, or the mif-application of the Publick Money: and yet I perfuade my felf, they would hardly allow fuch a proceeding, or commend it, as they do their own, to be wife and juftifiable.

They take fo much care of the Houfhold, that one would ordinarily fufpect they had fome Correfpondence with the difcontented Reforma-does of the *Green-Cloth*. I who live in the Country will never fpeak againft the fmell of Beef, no more than I will recommend that of Match to be at *White-Hall* inftead of it: But I am far from apprehending the Country Farmer to be concerned in the late Retrenchments; for ever fince the Tables were removed out of the Hall, and the Brewis turned into Fricaffees, they have loft their part in them, and efpecially fince the Kings coming in, not only the Country Farmer, but the Country Gentleman, and if you will the Country Lord too might have been fhrewdly difappointed if they had depended upon the Hofpitality of the White-Staves for a Dinner: That whole bufinefs was brought into fo unpopular a fhape, that the Nation will hardly take up Arms to reftore three or four Tables; they are rather pleafed to fee them put down, fince they were fo transformed, and wholly altered from their firft inftitution.

The Bankers are called the Bane of the Nation;

if fo, I have a great mind to believe, if it was poffible, it was for that reafon alone, the Earl of *Shaftsbury* broke them. I never was partial to that fort of men, and fo will leave them to make their own Apologies : but I muft fay, it feemeth a little hard to me to make thefe Pofitions, *The Bankers nor any body elfe muft lend the King Money. The Kings Wants are only to be fupplied by Parliament. The Parliament is not to give the King a farthing*. Thefe laid together, have in my judgment a very odd appearance : *Ay, but the King fhall have money enough upon good terms from the Parliament:* Shall he fo ? Thefe good terms are to come ; for thofe that have hitherto been offered are fo far from tempting, that they may rather fright the King from dealing with the fame Chapmen. Would thefe Gentlemen grow a little kinder and treat for a Mortgage of the Crown, allowing equity of Redemption, it might incline the King to hearken to them ; but by all that appeareth yet, we may conclude nothing lefs will fatisfie than a total furrender and paffing away his title to them.

In the cafe of 35 *Eliz.* it is pretended the Commons did not affume the power of fufpending Acts of Parliament : what was it then ? They did a thing they had a mind to in a manner they cannot juftifie ; they have as much right to make a Law, as they have fingly to declare what is Law : but becaufe they feem to give up the caufe by the flatnefs of their anfwer, I will only add, that as their zeal in this cafe tranfported them beyond their bounds, it is to be hoped, time and second thoughts will reduce them to a better temper against the next Meeting.

In Mr. *Fitz-harris's* Case it is said the Commons could not come to a Conference before they came to a Resolution: suppose it, what then? must that Resolution of necessity produce such Votes? If they had upon a cool Debate resolved that they were in the right, and sent to confer with the Lords either to have brought them to their opinion, or laid it aside if the Lords could have used arguments strong enough to convince them, they had prevented all objection. But to say the Commons could not resolve this amongst themselves without such injurious and unparliamentary terms as they were pleased to make use of in their Votes, is to say, if I have a difference with another man, and would discourse with him to compose it, I must needs for the better asserting my own right, send him word beforehand, he is a Rogue and a Villain, as a fitting Preliminary for a friendly Conference in order to an Agreement. For their Votes upon this occasion have, as much as in them lay, put the House of Lords under an Interdict, and fixed such a Character upon their whole Body, that if it were not a little sanctified by that chosen Remnant of Protesting Lords, I do not know but it might bear an Action, to be called by the Scandalous name of a Peer, after a Sentence that putteth all the Lords in as ill a condition as those few that in the former Parliament they bestowed their Votes upon. How much foever thefe Gentlemen may flatter themfelves in this matter, I can affure them, we in the Country underftand it otherwife than they would have us: for by the infinite heat and ftrugling to put off his Tryal both in and fince the Parliament, and by the Character of the Perfons who principally appear in it, we are apt to conclude fo warm a Contention muft be grounded upon fomething very confiderable; and we take it to be, that could this point be gained, men might either fpeak or act Treafon with impunity; and that would be of fuch excellent ufe to fome men, that no wonder if they are very earneft to compafs it.

I am very glad to hear there is nothing to be faid for thofe angry Men who have particular defigns; if any thing could have been faid, I am confident it might concern fome of thofe who have had a hand in this Paper, fo far as to have perfuaded them to venture at their Apology.

There is an Affertion made with the modefty and truth which belongeth to their Party, *viz.* *That all who are out of their places might have kept* *them.* If I am either rightly informed, or may be allowed to guefs from what they deferved, it is perhaps the only excufe thofe men have for their ill manners, that from the profpect they had of being turned out, they chofe to prevent the Kings Juftice, and to gain popularity, by endeavouring as much as in them lay to throw the affront upon him.

The Court hath long lain under the fcandal of

Popery, but it was news to me that they were for a Common-wealth too : This is fo very unlikely, that for the fake of our Religion which dependeth fo much upon their credit, I muſt give them warning to be a little more cautious in their Accufations, and take care that one part of their charge may agree with another; elfe as it happeneth to their *Mufti* Dr. *Oats*, men will be tempted by their alledging things impoſſible, to have doubts even of that part of their Evidence which may be true.

The laſt Paragraph telleth us *how we ſhall be happy, and the King be himſelf.* I was eager to know this receipt, having a great mind for my own fake, and for every bodies elfe, to have fuch a thing compaſſed ; but by taking the fenfe of the words as well as I can, it is no more than this in ſhort : All will be well if the King will be entirely governed by the Houfe of Commons; for we know they alone fignifie the Parliament, as they have more than once given us to underſtand by their Votes : and that their Advices are to be Commands, is no more a doubt, than that their Orders are to be Laws. I ſhall give no anfwer to this, but may be permitted to guefs the Kings will be *le Roy s'avifera.* In the mean time I have fo great a defire to be happy my felf, and that the Nation may be fo too, that if any thing may be received under the unwelcome name of Expedients, I would beg leave to offer a few to their better confideration.

I. *That no man who hath by notoriety of the fact within seven years last past promoted or connived at Popery, be thought now in earnest when he hawleth against it, or ever be admitted into Publick Employment.*

II. *That no man who hath Principles against all Kings, may pretend to advise Ours.*

III. *That none who would have Places for themselves, shall have any Vote to put others out of them.*

IV. *That none who have thought fit to leave the Council, should ever so disparage themselves as to return into it.*

V. *That none may ever be thought fit for Counsellors, or any other Employment, who have so little wit as to expect the Nation should be angry with the King, because they are afraid for themselves.*

VI. *That no Member of either House who in former Parliaments never consulted his Conscience, be now allowed to be a Martyr for it.*

VII. *That no man who is a known Ass in his own business, may be thought fit to meddle with the Kings.*

These things being granted, it is clearly my opinion, the King should stick at nothing the next Parliament can ask of him. Mens minds would be so quieted when they saw a Foundation laid of such impartial Justice, that we might hope for Peace and Union; and when the Vizzard of

Popularity is taken off, to fee *England* look like itfelf again. This is to be defired for many reafons; and befides thofe which relate to the Publick, I wifh it for a particular fatisfaction to my felf, who being void either of the ambition or the merit of pretending to any fhare in bufinefs, fhould think my felf very happy in the enjoyment of thofe mens Converfations, whofe Politicks I cannot fo well agree with, being confident that this would be a kind of Act of Exclufion upon thefe meafures, and that the greateft number of the complaining men would be at liberty and unemployed.

BIBLIOGRAPHY

I have included the separate editions of Halifax's
writings to 1700, when they were collected in
Miscellanies, two reprints of that volume and his
Character of King Charles the Second, etc., 1750. A
number of pamphlets, which I do not include,
have been attributed to Halifax. Most of these
were discussed and rejected by Miss Foxcroft
(II, 532–41). The internal evidence is, in varying
degrees, against his being the author of any of them.

1 [H.T.] (1) | [double rule] | OBSERVATIONS |
Upon a late LIBEL, called | *A Letter from a
Perſon of Quality to his* | *Friend, concerning the* | Kings
Declaration, &c [at the foot of B2ᵛ 'Printed for
C.M. 1681': some copies '*C. Maſon.* 1681.'].

Collation: 2°, A–B².

Contents: A1ʳ headed as above, followed by text to p. 8.

2a A | LETTER | TO A | DISSENTER, | Upon
occaſion of | HIS MAJESTIES | Late Gracious |
Declaration | OF | INDULGENCE.|| [single
square ornament]|| *LONDON:* | Printed for *G.H.*
1687.

Collation: 4°, A–B⁴ C².

Contents: A1ʳ title; A2ʳ–C2ʳ (pp. 1–17) text; C2ᵛ blank.

This edition appears to be the one most likely to have been
set up from a MS. It seems also to be the commonest.
H[enry] C[are] in his *Animadversions on A Late Paper
Entituled A Letter to a Dissenter,* 1687, says, 'printed it was
more than once or twice, and at last in a single sheet for
Conveniency of Postage'. 'A single sheet' presumably refers
to editions *2d–f.* The pamphlet is signed with the letters

'T. W.' of which no better explanation has been given than
that they stand for 'The Writer'. 'A Letter to a Dissenter
went about in the dark, and sold very deare, which was
answered by Sir Robert [*sic*] Lestrange; and both beinge
now printed, are publickly sold for 6*d*.' (Bramston's *Auto-
biography*, 1845, p. 299). It was probably published in
Aug. or early Sept. 1687, as it is mentioned as 'lately come
out' on 8 Sept. in the *Hatton Correspondence*; and one of
the many replies, *Remarks Upon a Pamphlet Stiled A Letter to
a Dissenter*, is dated 10 Sept. It was early suspected or
known to be by Halifax; see letter from Robert Harley,
8 Oct. 1687, *Hist. MSS. Com. Rept.* XIV (2), vol. III, p. 404.
Richard Baldwin entered *A Letter* in the *S.R.*, 11 May
1694. I have not found an edition of this year. He had
already reprinted it in *Fourteen Papers*...1689.

2*b* [Another edn.] Title-page as 2*a*, except that it has
    two ornaments.

    Collation: 4º, A² B⁴ C². The text ends on p. 17. C2ᵛ
    blank.

2*c* [Another edn.] Title-page as 2*a–b*, except that it has
    four ornaments.

    Collation: 4º, A⁴ B². The text is on pp. 1–10. The last
    eight lines are crowded and in small type.

2*d* [H.T.] 1 | A | LETTER | TO A | DISSENTER, |
    Upon occaſion of His Majeſties late Gracious De- |
    claration of Indulgence.

    Collation: 4º, A⁴.

    Contents: A1ʳ headed as above, followed by text to p. 8.

2*e* [H.T.] 1 | A | LETTER | TO A | DISSENTER, |
    Upon occaſion of His Majeſty's late Gracious |
    Declaration of Indulgence.

    Collation and Contents as 2*d*.

2*f* [H.T.] (1) | [double rule] | A | LETTER | TO A |
    DISSENTER, | Upon occaſion of His Majeſties late
    Gracious Declaration | of INDULGENCE.

    Collation: 4º, A⁴.

    Contents: A1ʳ headed as above, followed by text to p. 7.
    A4ᵛ blank.

2g LETTRE | ECRITE A UN | NONCONFORM-
ISTE, | *AU SUJET DE LA* | Derniére
Déclaration de | Sa Majefté, pour la | Tolérance. |
Traduite de L'ANGLOIS...A LONDRES, |
Imprimée pour G...H...1687.

Collation: 12°, A–B¹² C⁶, C6 blank?

2h [Another edn.] Title as above, except that there is no
publisher or place of printing. M.DC.LXXXVII.

Collation: A–B¹², B11 blank, B12 blank?

3a THE | Lady's New-years Gift: | OR, | ADVICE |
TO A | DAUGHTER, | Under thefe following
Heads: *Viz.*

Religion,	*Friendfhips,*
Husband,	*Cenfure,*
Children,	*Vanity* and
Servants,	*Affectation,*
Behaviour and	*Diverfions,*
Converfation,	*Dancing.*

|| *LONDON,* | Printed, and are to be fold by |
Randal Taylor near *Stationers* | *Hall.* 1688.

Collation: 12°, [A]² B–G¹² H⁸ I².

Contents: A1ᵛ LICENSED, *Jan.* 9. 168⅞. *Rob. Midgley*;
A2ʳ title; B1ʳ–I2ᵛ (pp. 1–164) the text.

Entered in the *S.R.* by Gillyflower and Partridge 12 Jan.
1688.

In the Advertisement printed in 3*b* Gillyflower and Partridge
say that the manuscript was sent to a scrivener, who sur-
reptitiously made for himself a copy which they bought
from a third person. They obtained a licence to print the
book as one by an unknown author, but finding, when it
was printed, that it had a multitude of faults, they got hold
of the 'Original Manuscript' for their new edition. The
right edition, they say, can be known by its 'Engraved
Figure'. Probably Gillyflower's and Partridge's names
were on the title-page of part of the edition. A B.M.
copy (721, b. 44) and my own are the only ones I have
seen: both have Randal Taylor's name alone. The text
is very bad. Halifax's surviving daughter, Elizabeth, was

born on 28 Aug. 1675. She would, therefore, have been thirteen and four months on New Year's Day, 1688. She married Lord Stanhope on 24 Feb. 1692. Their son, the fourth Earl of Chesterfield, the writer of the famous letters, was born on 22 Sept. 1694. His mother died 7 Sept. 1708.

3*b* THE | Lady's New-years Gift: | ... || *The Second Edition Corrected by the Original.* || *London*, Printed for *Matt. Gillyflower* | in *Weſtminſter-Hall*, and *James* | *Partridge* at *Charing-Croſs*. 1688.

Collation: 12°, [A]² B–G¹² H⁸ I² + engraved front. A2ʳ. Advertisement (see 3*a*).

T.C. Feb. 1688 'Printed for Matth. Gilliflower...and James Partridge...and sold by R. Taylor...'. On the title-page '*Houſe* and *Family*' are substituted for '*Children*', and '*Pride*' added between '*Affectation*' and '*Diverſions*'. This edition has been corrected throughout.

3*c* 'The Lady's New-years Gift...The Third Edition ...Twelves...Printed for Matth. Gilliflower... and James Partridge': entry in *T.C.* July 1688.

3*d* THE | LADIES | NEW-YEARS-GIFT:| ... | *The Third Edition* ... | *EDINBURGH*, | Printed by *John Reid*, for *James* | *Glen*, and *Walter Cunningham*. | MDCLXXXVIII.

Collation: 12°, A–K in eights and fours alternately + L⁴. The Advertisement is reprinted.

3*e* THE | Lady's New-year's Gift: | ... || 𝕿𝖍𝖊 𝕱𝖔𝖚𝖗𝖙𝖍 𝕰𝖉𝖎𝖙𝖎𝖔𝖓, 𝖊𝖝𝖆𝖈𝖙𝖑𝖞 𝕮𝖔𝖗𝖗𝖊𝖈𝖙𝖊𝖉. || *London*, Printed for *M.G.* and *J.P.* and are to | be ſold by *Thomas Chapman* at the *Golden* | *Key* at *Charing-Crofs*. 1692.

Collation: 12°, π1 (title-leaf) B–G¹² H⁸ I². There should doubtless be a frontispiece. The only copy I have seen lacks one.

3*f* ETRENNES | OU | CONSEILS | D'UN | HOMME | DE | QUALITE | A SA | FILLE. | *Traduit de l'Anglois* | [ornaments] | A LONDRES, | Chez Jaques Partridge à Charing-|Croſs &

MATIEU GILLIFLOWER | dans Weftminfter-
Hall. | [short rule] | M.DC.LXXXXII.

Collation: 8°, π⁴ A–H⁸ I².

Contents: π1ᵛ engraved front.; π2ʳ title-page; π3ʳᵛ AU
LECTEUR 'Ce Livre a paru en Anglois...'; π4ʳ
TABLE DES MATIERES; π4ᵛ 'Comme l'Imprimeur
d'entend pas le françois...' (24 errata).

This edition was printed in London. There are a few
footnotes on English customs, etc., to help French readers.

3*g* THE | Lady's New-years-Gift: | ... || 𝕿𝖍𝖊 𝕱𝖎𝖋𝖙𝖍
𝕰𝖉𝖎𝖙𝖎𝖔𝖓 𝖊𝖝𝖆𝖈𝖙𝖑𝖞 𝕮𝖔𝖗𝖗𝖊𝖈𝖙𝖊𝖉. || ... || *London*, Printed
for *M. Gillyflower* and are to | be fold by *Francis
Wright*...1696.

Collation: 12°, π1 (title-leaf) B–G¹² H⁸ I².

The B.M. copy has no front.: no doubt there should be
one.

3*h* ADVICE | TO A | DAUGHTER, | ... || 𝕿𝖍𝖊
𝕾𝖎𝖝𝖙𝖍 𝕰𝖉𝖎𝖙𝖎𝖔𝖓. || To which is added | THE |
CHARACTER | OF A | TRIMMER, | ... ||
By the late Noble *M.* of *H.* || Printed for *M.
Gillyflower* and *B.* | *Tooke*, 1699. [enclosed within
double rules].

Collation and Contents: 12°, front.; π1ʳ general title as
above; A1ʳ [sub title-page] THE CHARACTER OF
A TRIMMER...1699 (see 4*f*); A2–A12, B–D¹²
E¹⁰ Preface and text; χ1ʳ [sub title-page] THE Lady's
New-years-Gift: ... 𝕿𝖍𝖊 𝕾𝖎𝖝𝖙𝖍 𝕰𝖉𝖎𝖙𝖎𝖔𝖓, ... 1699;
²B–G¹² H⁸ I² text.

4*a* THE | CHARACTER | OF A | TRIMMER. |
HIS | OPINION | OF | I. The Laws and
Government. | II. Proteftant Religion. | III. The
Papifts. | IV. Foreign Affairs. || By the
Honourable Sir *W. C.* || *LONDON*, | Printed in
the Year, M DC LXXXVIII [enclosed within
double rules].

Collation: 4°, A–F⁴.

Contents: A1^r title; A2^{rv} The PREFACE; A3^r–F4^r (pp. 1–43) the text.

The Character of a Trimmer, which was no doubt intended for the eyes of Charles II, was probably written at the end of 1684. A 'Trimmer' had taken the place of a Whig as an interlocutor in *The Observator* on 13 Nov. 1682 and his 'Character and Humour' had been given by L'Estrange, with his usual vigour, in the numbers for 3 and 4 Dec. 1684. L'Estrange's onslaught may have been the immediate cause of Halifax's defence of a 'Trimmer's' position. MS. copies were in circulation before 26 Jan. 1685, when Sir W. Coventry wrote to Lord Weymouth denying that he was the author (Foxcroft, II, 274). Coventry does, in fact, in his letter say of a 'Trimmer' that he is one 'who would sitt upright and not overturne the boate', but he and his nephew were on intimate terms and the metaphor may have arisen in conversation between them. To Coventry has been frequently ascribed *Englands Appeal from the Private Cabal at White-Hall to the Great Council of the Nation*, 1673, but if he wrote it, which is doubtful, it is very different in style from *The Character of a Trimmer*. Coventry is given as the author on the title-pages of 4*a–c*, but Halifax, it will be noticed, on the title-page of 4*d*. Richard Baldwin in 1697 supposed that Coventry was the writer, but that the early printed text had been corrected by Halifax (see 4*e*). When the sheets were reissued two years later (4*f*) the Marquis was substituted for Coventry. In *Saviliana* it is explained that the piece went under Coventry's name 'because the printer workt from a copy which was found amongst Sr William's papers'. Coventry died on 23 June 1686 and his library was sold in May 1687 (Bodl. Wood E. 20). The first edition was published before 10 May 1688 (see the second Earl of Chesterfield's *Letters*, 1829, p. 331). Richard Baldwin, who published 4*b*, may have been responsible for 4*a*, but he would no doubt have been unable to obtain a licence for the pamphlet before the Revolution. 4*a* must have been set up from a very bad MS. A good illustration of the differences in the texts of 4*a–e* occurs in some words in a sentence on p. 34 of 4*a*. Here they read 'he broach'd his Intentions upon a Cost'. This being nonsense they were altered in 4*b* to 'he broached his Intentions of several new Claims'. In 4*e* what was no doubt the right reading was given, 'he broach'd his Pretensions upon *Alost*'. In 4*d* it is 'he broached his pretentions upon *A Lost*'. None of the early printed texts is satisfactory. For the available MSS. see Foxcroft, II.

4*b* THE | CHARACTER | OF A | TRIMMER. | ... || By the Honourable, Sir *W. Coventry*. || The Second Edition, carefully Corrected, and cleared | from the Errors of the firſt Impreſſion. || *Licenſed* December 27. 1688. || *LONDON*, | Printed for 𝕽𝖎𝖈𝖍𝖆𝖗𝖉 𝕭𝖆𝖑𝖉𝖜𝖎𝖓, next the *Black Bull* in | the *Old-Bailey*, MDCLXXXIX. [enclosed within double rules].

Collation: 4°, A–F⁴.

Entered in the *S.R.* 29 Dec. 1688. There are corrections in this edition, but they may have been made by the publisher or printer.

4*c* THE | CHARACTER | OF A | TRIMMER, | ... || The Third Edition ... || 𝕷𝖎𝖈𝖊𝖓𝖘𝖊𝖉 𝖆𝖓𝖉 𝕰𝖓𝖙𝖗𝖊𝖉 𝖆𝖈𝖈𝖔𝖗𝖉𝖎𝖓𝖌 𝖙𝖔 𝕺𝖗𝖉𝖊𝖗. || *LONDON*, | Printed for 𝕽𝖎𝖈𝖍𝖆𝖗𝖉 𝕭𝖆𝖑𝖉𝖜𝖎𝖓,...MDCLXXXIX.

Collation: 4°, A–E⁴.

This edition, which is in smaller type than 4*a–b*, is a reprint of 4*b*.

4*d* THE | CHARACTER | OF A | TRIMMER | Concerning | RELIGION, LAWS and LIBER-TIES. || By a Perſon of Honour, Mſs. H. || [ornament] || *LONDON*, | Printed in the Year, MDCLXXXIX.

Collation: 4°, A⁴ B² C–F⁴ G².

On p. 47 below FINIS is the following: 'INTELLIGENT READER, If this be pleasant to thy Taste, Expect two such Dishes from the said Author; *viz. REASONS against Repealing the Acts of Parliament concerning the TEST.* The other, *A Letter to a* Dissenter, &c.' This is a poorly printed edition: the text is manifestly corrupt, but it was apparently set up from a different MS. from that used for 4*a*. It certainly gives one correct reading where 4*a–c* and *e* are wrong and it may give others. The only copy I have seen belongs to Professor D. Nichol Smith.

4*e* THE | CHARACTER | OF A | TRIMMER. | ... || By the Honourable Sir *W. Coventry.* | Corrected and Amended by a | Perſon of Honour. || 𝔗𝔥𝔢 𝔗𝔥𝔦𝔯𝔡 𝔈𝔡𝔦𝔱𝔦𝔬𝔫. || *LONDON,* | Printed for *Rich. Baldwin,* near the | *Oxford-Arms* in *Warwick-lane,* 1697. [enclosed within double rules].

Collation: 12°, A¹² (+ π² inserted between A1 and A2) B–D¹² E¹⁰.

Contents: A1ʳ title-page ; π1ʳ–π2ᵛ ADVERTISEMENT ; A2ʳ–A4ᵛ THE PREFACE; A5ʳ–E10ʳ (pp. 1–105) the text, E10ᵛ blank.

The writer of the Advertisement, after stating that the piece 'is the Product of Sir William Coventry's Contemplations' says that 'it stands obliged to the great care of the late M. of Hallifax, who ... with his own Pen deliver'd it from innumerable Mistakes and Errors that stuff'd and crouded the former Edition'. The text, though none too carefully printed, contains corrections and alterations (see 4*a*). Halifax's use of 'th' for the third person singular, which is reproduced in 4*a–d*, is generally modernised in 4*e*. This text was reprinted in 10*a*.

4*f* The sheets of 4*e* were used in making up 3*h*, where the Advertisement is omitted and the following title-leaf substituted for that in 4*e*: THE | CHARACTER | OF A | TRIMMER, | ... || By the late Noble *M.* of *H.* || The 𝔗𝔥𝔦𝔯𝔡 𝔈𝔡𝔦𝔱𝔦𝔬𝔫. || *LONDON,* | Printed for *M. Gillyflower* and | *B. Tooke,* 1699.

5 [H.T.] (1) | [double rule] | THE | ANATOMY | OF AN | EQUIVALENT.

Collation: 4°: A–B⁴.

Contents: A1ʳ headed as above, followed by text to p. 16.

On p. 16 of some copies the last sentence has no inverted commas and 𝔄𝔫𝔤𝔢𝔯 is divided between two lines: in others there are inverted commas and 𝔄𝔫𝔤𝔢𝔯 is on one line. 'There lately appears from hand to hand a new pamphlet called *The Anatomy of an Equivalent,* which makes a great noise, and is censured according to each man's passion: it is very sharp and biting, though the application be veiled

over and is said to be writ by a noble peer!' (11 Sept.
1688, *Ellis Correspondence*, 11, 172). Lady Russell mentions
it on 7 Oct. 1688 as 'the newest good paper I know'. *The
Anatomy of an Equivalent; By the Marqueſs of Halifax,
Adapted to the Equivalent in the present Articles*, 1706 (A⁴),
probably printed at Edinburgh, adapts Halifax's tract to
the 'Equivalents' offered Scotland at the time of the Union.

6 ESSAYS | OF | ... | MONTAIGNE. | ... ||
To which is added a ſhort Character of the | Author
and Tranſlator, by way of Let-|ter; Written by
a Perſon of Honour. || Now rendred into Engliſh |
By *CHARLES COTTON*, Eſq: || ... || The
𝔉irſt 𝔙olume. || *LONDON*, | Printed for *T.
Baſſet...M. Gilliflower* and *W. Henſman...*
1693.

The second edition of Cotton's Montaigne. A dedication
to Halifax had been printed in the first (1685), and to
this was added an 'Advertisement' signed 'T. B.' and
'M. G.' and a letter from Halifax to Cotton 'at his House
in Berisford. To be left at Ashburne in Derby-shire.'
Though referred to on the title-page the Letter and
Advertisement, which were printed on four leaves signed
*1–[4], are found in some copies only.

7 [H.T.] The following Maxims were found
amongſt | the Papers of the Great *Almanzor*; and
tho they may loſe | a good deal of their Original
Spirit by the Tranſlation, | yet they ſeem to be ſo
Applicable to all Times, that it is | thought no
Diſſervice to make them Publick.

Collation: Iᵒ, on verso of leaf 'Printed in the year
MDCXCIII'.

Copies: Guildhall Library (Tracts Z. 83) Bodl. (Wood
276ᴀ(19) 13¼″ × 7¾″). Wood added in MS. after the date,
'Sept'. The sheet contains 33 maxims numbered i–xxxiii.
They were reprinted in 10*a–c*. They were also reprinted,
with the heading and date in *State Tracts*, vol. 11, 1706.
For a discussion of the authorship of other collections of
'Maxims of State', printed and in MS., see Foxcroft, 11,
447. The 64 'Maxims of State' in *The Second Volume of*

Miscellaneous Works of George Duke of Buckingham, 1705, are different from the 33 Maxims of 7 and 10. Fourteen are ascribed to Charles Montague in B.M. Add. MSS. 6703, f. 26, and 32,095, f. 406, both of which contain the Marquis's 33 Maxims.

8   A | Rough Draught | OF A | NEW MODEL | AT | SEA. || [8 ornaments] || *LONDON*, | Printed for *A. Banks*. 1694. [enclosed within double rules].

Collation: 4°, A–D⁴.

Contents: A1ʳ title; A2ʳ–D3ᵛ (pp. 3–30) text; D4 blank. Richard Baldwin entered *A Rough Draught* in the *S.R.* 11 May 1694.

It is uncertain when this tract, which, as Miss Foxcroft says, is obviously a portion of a work designed on a larger scale, was written. The question of the relative merits of 'Tarpaulins' and gentlemen as officers, was an old one (Pepys, 20 Oct. 1666), and it is possible, from an expression which appears to mean that he was not a member of either House, that Halifax had written the piece during the Dutch War of 1665–7. If so, it must have been revised before being sent to press in 1694. The date of entry in the *S.R.* strengthens Miss Foxcroft's suggestion that it was printed in connection with the debates on Naval affairs early in 1694. There is a MS. in the Bodleian (Rawl. D. 380, f. 207) which Miss Foxcroft believes to be earlier than the printed text.

9   SOME|CAUTIONS|Offered to the|CONSIDER-ATION | Of Thoſe who are to | Chuſe MEMBERS | To SERVE in the | 𝔈nſuing 𝔓arliament. | [double rule]|*LONDON:*|Printed in the Year MDCXCV. [enclosed within double rules].

Collation: 4°, A–D⁴.

Contents: A1ʳ title; A2ʳ–D4ᵛ (pp. 3–32) the text.

There are two editions or states. CAUTIONS on the title-page of one covers $3\frac{9}{16}''$: on the other it covers 4″. Small changes were made in the text. On p. 18, l. 17 ends with the words 'will be the Honester' in some copies: in others 'if he hath neaver so much'. These additional words are found with both title-pages. Ralph (*Hist. of England,* II, 608) says that 'During the whole time of the Election the Press was as fruitful as the Mud of *Nilus*...every Day produc'd some Effort, either to raise or lay the Spirit of Opposition: And of Those the most remarkable is the Tract said to be written by the Marquis of *Hallifax* under the title of *Some Cautions* ...'. Halifax died on 5 April 1695 and the pamphlet is believed to have been written during the last few months of his life in anticipation of a General Election which, in fact, took place in October.

10*a* Miscellanies | BY | The Right Noble LORD, | The Late Lord Marquefs | OF | HALIFAX. | VIZ. | I. *Advice to a* DAUGHTER. | II. *The Character of a* TRIMMER. | III. *The Anatomy of an* EQUIVALENT. | IV. *A Letter to a* DISSENTER. | V. *Cautions for Choice of* PARLIA-|MENT MEN. | VI. *A Rough Draught of a* NEW MO-|DEL *at* SEA. | VII. *Maxims of* STATE, *&c.* || LONDON: | Printed for *Matt. Gillyflower* at the *Spread-|Eagle* in *Weftminfter-Hall.* 1700. [enclosed within double rules].

Collation: π1 (title leaf) A^8 a (3 ll.) B–P^8 Q1–3 ^{x}Q^8 q^8 [R] 4–8 S–X^8 Y^4. Some copies have also an engraved front. before *Advice to a Daughter*, probably printed from the plate prepared for *3e*.

This collation gives the make-up of the volume in its final form. *A Letter to a Dissenter from his Friend at the Hague,* which had been printed separately and in *Fourteen Papers*, 1689, and which is not by Halifax, was at first included and occupied sigs. Q4–R3. When the mistake was discovered Halifax's *Letter* was printed on two sheets, which were given the sigs. Q and q. In some copies these were added after Y without *A Letter from the Hague* being cancelled. But in most the leaves carrying the wrong *Letter* were cut out and those carrying the right put in their place. The catch letter 'A' on Q3^{v} happened to be correct for either *Letter*. Sigs. A and a, on which are printed *Sacellum Apollinare*, are sometimes placed at the end of the volume. The sub titles to *The Character* (G 3) and to *Some Cautions* (R 4) are dated 1699, those to *A Letter to a Dissenter* (ˣQ 1), *A Rough Draught* (U 3) and *Maxims* (X 7) 1700. Y 3–4 carry the Advertisement and Letter to Cotton (see no. 6). The pieces are separately paged. A B.M. copy (12273, b. 1) which has both *Letters* has a different title-page from that given above: Miſcellanies | By the Late Right Noble Lord | Marqueſs of *HALIFAX*. | ... || [9 ornaments] || ... Printed for *Matt. Gillyflower* ... 1700. There are other typographical differences.

S.R. 14 Dec. 1699. *T.C.* Feb. 1700.
Sacellum Apollinare. A Funeral Poem to the Memory of ...
George, Late Marquiſs of Hallifax, 1695 (2°) has been attributed to Settle.

In her Preface, Miss Foxcroft refers to and, in different parts of her two volumes reprints, a MS. entitled *Saviliana* (some account of the books and their authors, see *Hist. MSS. Com. Rept.* II, Ap.). This may have been written by William Mompesson (1639–1709, *D.N.B.*), at one time Halifax's chaplain. *Saviliana* was clearly intended as a preface to an edition of Halifax's tracts, possibly 10*a*.

10*b* Miſcellanies | BY | The Late Lord Marquis | OF | HALIFAX. | ... || *LONDON* : | Printed for *W. Rogers* ... *Benj. Tooke* ... and *D. Midwinter* and *T. Leigh* ... 1704.

Collation: 8°, π² B–Z⁸ Aa⁶, π1 blank: continuous pagination: five sub titles. *Sacellum Apollinare* occupies Z5–Aa6.

10*c* MISCELLANIES | ... || *The* THIRD EDITION. || ... Printed for B. TOOKE, ... D. MIDWINTER, ... and J. HOOKE, ... M DCC XVII.

Collation: 12°, A–N¹².

11 A | CHARACTER | OF | KING *CHARLES* | THE SECOND : | AND | POLITICAL, MORAL *and* MISCELLANEOUS | THOUGHTS *and* REFLECTIONS. || By *GEORGE SAVILE,* | MARQUIS of HALIFAX. | [double rule] | *LONDON:* | Printed for J. and R. TONSON and S. DRAPER | in the *Strand.* M DCC L.

Collation: 8°, A⁴ B–M⁸ N⁴.

Contents: A1ʳ title; A2ʳ ADVERTISEMENT 'The following Character of King Charles the Second, with the Political, Moral and Miscellaneous Thoughts... were written by George Savile Marquis of Halifax, and were taken from his original Manuscripts, in the Possession of his Grand-daughter Dorothy Countess of Burlington'; A3ʳ–A4ᵛ CONTENTS; B1ʳ–E6ʳ (pp. 1–59) text of the Character; D7ᵛ half-title; E8ʳ–N4ʳ (pp. 63–183) text of Thoughts, etc.

The second Marquis of Halifax, who died 31 Aug. 1700, married a daughter of the Earl of Nottingham. Their daughter Dorothy (1699–1758) married Richard Boyle, Earl of Burlington. Nottingham and Lady Burlington are traditionally supposed to have destroyed some memoirs or journals kept by Halifax (see Foxcroft, I, viii and Malone's *Dryden*, II, 209).

12 *Bishop Burnet's History of His Own Time*, Vol. II. 1734.

On pp. 725–6 is printed a character of Burnet said, in the margin, to be by the Marquis of Halifax.

For EU product safety concerns, contact us at Calle de José Abascal, 56–1°, 28003 Madrid, Spain or eugpsr@cambridge.org.

www.ingramcontent.com/pod-product-compliance
Ingram Content Group UK Ltd.
Pitfield, Milton Keynes, MK11 3LW, UK
UKHW030913160425
457438UK00001B/2